Stock Market USA Book for Beginners

Investing Guide for Learning & Understanding the Basics

By Brian Mahoney

Table of Contents

Disclaimer

The information provided in this book is for educational purposes only and should not be considered as financial or investment advice. The strategies, techniques, and opinions shared here are based on general knowledge and personal experience. Investing in the stock market involves risk, including the potential loss of principal. Past performance is not indicative of future results.

The author, publisher, and any associated parties are not responsible for any investment decisions made based on the information in this book. Before making any financial decisions, readers should consult with a qualified financial advisor or do their own thorough research to ensure that their investment choices align with their financial goals and risk tolerance.

By using this book, you acknowledge that you understand the risks involved in investing and that any action taken based on the content provided is solely at your own discretion.

Introduction

Welcome to the world of stock market investing, where opportunities for financial growth and independence await those willing to learn, plan, and take action. Whether you're here because you're tired of watching your savings grow at a snail's pace in a traditional bank account, or because you've heard success stories of people who've built wealth by investing in the stock market, this book is your gateway to a better financial future.

If the idea of investing seems overwhelming—filled with cryptic jargon, fluctuating graphs, and intimidating risks—you're not alone. Many beginners feel the same way at first. However, with the right guidance and a solid understanding of the basics, you'll soon realize that the stock market is not as mysterious as it seems. In fact, it's one of the most accessible and proven methods of building long-term wealth, regardless of your starting point.

This book is designed specifically for beginners like you. Our mission is to break down the seemingly complex world of investing into manageable, practical steps that you can take immediately. You don't need a degree in finance or a background in economics to get started. All you need is curiosity, commitment, and a willingness to learn.

Here's what you can expect as we embark on this journey together:

Foundational Knowledge: You'll learn the core principles of how the stock market works, why companies issue stocks, and how investors like you can benefit.

Clear Strategies: We'll explore various types of investments—like individual stocks, mutual funds, ETFs, and more—so you can make informed decisions based on your goals and risk tolerance.

Tools and Techniques: From understanding financial statements to using trading platforms, you'll gain the practical skills to confidently navigate the market.

Mindset for Success: Successful investing isn't just about numbers—it's about discipline, patience, and a long-term perspective. We'll discuss how to develop the right mindset to stay on track.

Above all, this book emphasizes simplicity. You don't need to chase every new trend or day trade obsessively to succeed. Instead, you'll learn time-tested strategies that focus on steady, sustainable growth. Investing is a marathon, not a sprint, and this book will equip you with the tools to stay the course and achieve your financial goals.

By the end of this book, you'll not only understand the mechanics of the stock market but also feel confident in taking your first steps as an investor. Whether you're looking to build a retirement fund, save for a major life event, or simply grow your wealth, the knowledge you gain here will serve as your foundation for success.

So, let's get started. Your journey toward financial empowerment begins now.

Chapter 1:
The Foundations of
the Stock Market

1.1 What is the Stock Market?

Definition: A marketplace where buyers and sellers trade shares of publicly held companies.

Purpose: Helps businesses raise capital while providing investors opportunities to earn returns.

Analogy: The stock market as a supermarket for company ownership.

1.2 How the Stock Market Operates

Stock Exchanges: Centralized platforms like the New York Stock Exchange (NYSE) and NASDAQ where trading happens.

Participants in the Market:

Investors: Individuals, institutions, and governments.

Brokers: Middlemen connecting buyers and sellers.

Market Makers: Entities ensuring liquidity by constantly quoting buy and sell prices.

Trading Hours: Typical stock market trading schedules (e.g., 9:30 AM to 4:00 PM ET in the U.S.).

1.3 Key Concepts to Know

Shares: Units of ownership in a company.

Stock Prices: Determined by supply, demand, and investor sentiment.

Market Capitalization: The total value of a company's shares, indicating its size.

Indices: Benchmarks like the S&P 500, Dow Jones, and NASDAQ Composite that track overall market performance.

1.4 Why Companies Go Public

Initial Public Offering (IPO): A company's first sale of stock to the public to raise funds.

Advantages for Companies: Access to capital for growth, debt repayment, or acquisitions.

What It Means for Investors: IPOs as opportunities to buy into early-stage growth.

1.5 Types of Stock Markets

Primary Market: Where new stocks are issued (e.g., during an IPO).
Secondary Market: Where previously issued stocks are traded among investors.

1.6 The Players in the Stock Market

Retail Investors: Everyday individuals buying stocks through brokers or online platforms.
Institutional Investors: Large organizations like pension funds, mutual funds, and hedge funds.
Regulators: Bodies like the Securities and Exchange Commission (SEC) ensuring fair and transparent practices.

1.7 Historical Perspective on the Stock Market

The Origins: Early stock trading in Amsterdam and the establishment of the NYSE in 1792.
Major Milestones: The Great Depression, dot-com bubble, and financial crises shaping modern investing.
Technological Evolution: From floor trading to high-speed digital transactions.

1.8 Why the Stock Market Matters to You

Personal Financial Growth: Building wealth over time through compounding.
Economic Indicator: Reflecting the health of industries and economies.
Access to Innovation: Investing in cutting-edge industries and startups shaping the future.

1.9 Dispelling Common Myths

"The stock market is just gambling."
Counterpoint: Investing is based on research and strategy, unlike games of chance.

"You need to be rich to invest."
Counterpoint: Platforms now allow starting with as little as $5.

"It's too complicated for beginners."
Counterpoint: Education and simple strategies make it accessible.

Conclusion:

By understanding the foundations of the stock market, you're taking the first step toward becoming a confident investor. The next chapter will explore the benefits and risks, helping you decide how investing aligns with your goals.

Chapter 2:
The Benefits and
Risks of Investing

2.1 The Potential Rewards of Investing

Investing in the stock market can provide significant advantages when approached wisely:

Wealth Building Over Time:

Example: Historical average returns of 7-10% per year for the S&P 500.
Explanation of how compound interest amplifies returns over decades.

Beating Inflation:

Why saving alone isn't enough; the stock market helps preserve and grow purchasing power.

Income Generation:

Dividend-paying stocks as a source of passive income.

Ownership in Businesses:

How buying shares makes you a part-owner of the company, benefiting from its success.

Flexibility and Liquidity:

Stocks can be sold at market value, offering liquidity compared to other investments like real estate.

2.2 Understanding the Risks of Stock Market Investing

Every opportunity comes with potential downsides. Awareness and preparation are key:

Market Volatility:

Prices can rise and fall sharply due to news, economic conditions, or investor sentiment.

Example: Drops during events like the 2008 financial crisis or 2020 pandemic.
Company-Specific Risks:
Poor management, competition, or scandals can cause individual stocks to plummet.
Economic Risks:
Recessions, interest rate changes, and geopolitical events affecting entire sectors or markets.
Liquidity Risk:
Some smaller stocks may be hard to sell quickly without impacting their price.
Emotional Investing:
Fear and greed leading to poor decisions, like panic selling during market downturns.

2.3 Balancing Risk and Reward

The Risk-Return Tradeoff:

Higher potential returns often come with higher risks.

Example: Comparing safer blue-chip stocks to high-risk speculative stocks.
The Role of Time:

How long-term investing smooths out short-term volatility.

Emphasis on patience and discipline.

Diversification as a Shield:

Spreading investments across industries and asset classes to reduce risk.

2.4 Managing Risk Effectively

Actionable strategies to minimize exposure to losses:

Asset Allocation:

Distributing investments among stocks, bonds, and cash based on your goals and risk tolerance.

Portfolio Diversification:

Avoiding concentration in one stock, sector, or geography.
Example: A balanced portfolio with technology, healthcare, consumer goods, and energy stocks.

Setting Stop-Loss Orders:

Automating sales if stock prices drop to a pre-set level to limit losses.

Avoiding Leverage:

Risks of borrowing money to invest.

Educating Yourself:

Staying informed about the market and ongoing trends.

2.5 Aligning Risk with Your Personal Profile

Risk Tolerance Assessment:
Questions to determine if you're conservative, moderate, or aggressive.
Example: How would you feel if your portfolio dropped 20% in a week?
Life Stage Considerations:
Younger investors may take more risks for long-term growth.
Retirees may prioritize stability and income.

2.6 Case Studies: Balancing Risk and Reward

Success Story:

A young investor using index funds to build wealth over 30 years.

Cautionary Tale:

A speculative trader losing money by chasing "hot tips" without research.

Conclusion:

Investing in the stock market offers tremendous rewards but comes with inherent risks. Understanding these risks and how to manage them equips you to make informed, confident decisions. The next chapter will guide you in setting up a strong foundation for investing, starting with clear goals and the right tools.

Chapter 3: Setting Up for Success

3.1 Defining Your Financial Goals

Before investing, it's crucial to establish clear objectives. Consider these common goals:

Short-Term Goals: Saving for a car, vacation, or emergency fund (timeframe: 1-3 years).

Investment types: High-yield savings accounts or conservative ETFs.

Medium-Term Goals: Buying a home, funding education, or starting a business (timeframe: 3-10 years).

Investment types: Balanced mix of stocks and bonds.

Long-Term Goals: Retirement or wealth building (timeframe: 10+ years).

Investment types: Broad-based index funds, growth stocks, and dividend-paying stocks.

Action Step: Write down your goals with timelines to clarify your investment purpose.

3.2 Assessing Your Risk Tolerance

Understanding how much risk you're comfortable taking is key to building a portfolio that suits you:

Risk Tolerance Levels:

Conservative: Prioritize preserving capital with lower returns.

Moderate: Willing to accept moderate risk for balanced growth.

Aggressive: Comfortable with volatility for higher potential returns.

Factors Influencing Risk Tolerance:

Age: Younger investors typically have higher risk tolerance due to longer time horizons.

Income stability and financial obligations: Stable income allows for higher risk.

Personality: How you handle stress during market downturns.

Action Step: Take a risk tolerance quiz to gauge your comfort level.

3.3 Establishing an Emergency Fund

Before investing, ensure you have a financial safety net:

Why It's Essential: Protects you from needing to sell investments during emergencies.

How Much to Save: 3-6 months of living expenses in a highly liquid, low-risk account.

Where to Keep It: High-yield savings accounts or money market funds.

Action Step: Calculate your monthly expenses and start building your emergency fund if you don't already have one.

3.4 Choosing the Right Brokerage Account

Your brokerage account is your gateway to the stock market. Key considerations:

Types of Accounts:

Standard Brokerage Account: Offers flexibility with no restrictions on withdrawals.

Retirement Accounts: Tax-advantaged accounts like IRAs or 401(k)s for long-term goals.

Features to Look For:

Low fees and commissions

User-friendly platforms

Access to research tools and educational resources

Customer service availability

Popular Online Brokers for Beginners:

Fidelity, Charles Schwab, TD Ameritrade, Robinhood, and E*TRADE.

Action Step: Compare brokerages and choose one that aligns with your needs.

3.5 Understanding Initial Investment Requirements

Starting Small: Many brokers allow you to begin with as little as $5 using fractional shares.

Budgeting for Investments: Allocate a percentage of your income, such as 10-20%, for investing.

Avoiding Overextension: Only invest what you can afford to lose without impacting your essential expenses.

Action Step: Decide on your initial investment amount and set a monthly contribution goal.

3.6 Building the Right Mindset for Success

Successful investing requires more than money; it requires the right mindset:

Patience: Understand that wealth-building takes time.

Discipline: Stick to your strategy, even during market fluctuations.

Continuous Learning: Stay curious and informed about market trends and strategies.

Emotional Control: Avoid impulsive decisions driven by fear or greed.

Action Step: Commit to long-term thinking by writing down affirmations about your investment journey.

3.7 Setting Up Automatic Contributions

Automating your investments simplifies the process and ensures consistency:

Benefits:

Removes the temptation to time the market.

Builds wealth steadily over time.

How to Automate:

Set up recurring transfers from your bank to your brokerage account.

Use robo-advisors for automated portfolio management.

Action Step: Set up an automated monthly transfer to your brokerage account.

3.8 Tracking Progress and Adjusting Goals

Your financial goals and circumstances may change over time. Regular reviews help keep you on track:

Track Portfolio Performance: Compare returns to your target benchmarks.

Revisit Goals: Adjust timelines or contributions as needed.

Stay Flexible: Be ready to pivot strategies based on life changes.

Action Step: Schedule quarterly check-ins to review your goals and portfolio.

Conclusion:

By setting clear goals, preparing financially, and choosing the right tools, you're establishing a strong foundation for stock market success. The next chapter will dive into the various investment types available to help you diversify and optimize your portfolio.

Chapter 4:
Types of
Investments in the
Stock Market

4.1 Common Stock

Definition: A share representing ownership in a company, with voting rights at shareholder meetings.

Key Features:

Offers potential for capital appreciation as the company grows.

May pay dividends, but not guaranteed.

Example: Apple (AAPL) or Tesla (TSLA).

Pros:

High growth potential.

Voting rights give shareholders a say in major company decisions.
Cons:

Greater risk of price volatility.

Dividend payments may fluctuate or cease during financial hardships.

4.2 Preferred Stock

Definition: A type of stock that offers fixed dividend payments and priority over common stockholders in the event of liquidation.

Key Features:

Typically does not provide voting rights.

More stable income compared to common stock.

Pros:

Reliable dividend income.

Lower volatility than common stock.

Cons:

Limited growth potential compared to common stock.

Less liquidity in the market.

4.3 Exchange-Traded Funds (ETFs)

Definition: Investment funds that trade on stock exchanges, holding a diversified portfolio of assets.

Key Features:

Tracks indices (e.g., S&P 500), sectors, or specific themes.

Example: SPDR S&P 500 ETF (SPY) or Vanguard Total Stock Market ETF (VTI).

Pros:

Instant diversification.

Low expense ratios and management fees.

Easy to buy and sell like individual stocks.

Cons:

No control over the individual assets in the fund.

Limited potential for outsized gains compared to individual stock-picking.

4.4 Mutual Funds

Definition: Investment funds pooling money from multiple investors to invest in a professionally managed portfolio of assets.

Key Features:

Actively managed by fund managers.

Example: Fidelity Contrafund or Vanguard 500 Index Fund.

Pros:

Professional management simplifies investing.

Diversification reduces risk.

Cons:

Higher fees compared to ETFs.

Fund performance may not consistently beat the market.

4.5 Index Funds

Definition: A type of mutual fund or ETF that tracks a specific market index, like the S&P 500 or NASDAQ.

Key Features:

Passively managed to mirror the performance of the index.

Pros:

Extremely low fees.

Historically reliable returns over the long term.

Cons:

Limited to the performance of the index it tracks.

No flexibility to adjust holdings during market changes.

4.6 Dividend-Paying Stocks

Definition: Shares of companies that regularly distribute a portion of their profits to shareholders as dividends.

Key Features:

Examples: Coca-Cola (KO) or Procter & Gamble (PG).

Dividends may be reinvested to compound growth.

Pros:

Reliable income stream, even during market downturns.

Potential for both income and capital appreciation.

Cons:

Dividend payments are not guaranteed.

Lower growth potential compared to high-growth stocks.

4.7 Growth Stocks

Definition: Stocks of companies expected to grow earnings at an above-average rate compared to the market.

Key Features:

Examples: Amazon (AMZN) or Nvidia (NVDA).

Often reinvest profits into expansion rather than paying dividends.

Pros:

High potential for significant capital gains.

Represents innovative, high-performing industries.

Cons:

Greater risk and volatility.

Returns may take years to materialize.

4.8 Value Stocks

Definition: Stocks trading at a lower price relative to their fundamentals (e.g., earnings, dividends).

Key Features:

Examples: JPMorgan Chase (JPM) or Berkshire Hathaway (BRK.A).

Often mature companies with steady earnings.

Pros:

Potential for price appreciation as the market "corrects" undervaluation.

Lower downside risk compared to speculative stocks.

Cons:

Growth may be slower than market averages.

Requires patience to see returns.

4.9 Sector-Specific Investments

Definition: Focused investments in specific industries like technology, healthcare, energy, or real estate.

Key Features:

Examples: Technology ETFs or Real Estate Investment Trusts (REITs).

Pros:

Allows targeting of high-growth or high-demand sectors.

Enhances portfolio diversification.

Cons:

Concentrated risk in one sector.

Vulnerable to industry-specific downturns.

4.10 Balancing Your Portfolio with Different Types

Why Diversification Matters: Spreading your investments across types reduces overall risk.

Example Portfolio Allocation for Beginners:

60% in index funds or ETFs.

20% in dividend-paying stocks.

10% in growth stocks.

10% in sector-specific investments.

Action Step: Start by selecting 1-2 investment types that match your goals and gradually expand as you gain confidence.

Conclusion:

Understanding the different types of stock market investments is the first step in creating a well-rounded portfolio. The next chapter will teach you how to develop strategies for combining these investments to suit your personal goals and risk tolerance.

Chapter 5:
Building Your
Investment
Strategy

5.1 The Importance of Having a Strategy

Investing without a clear plan is like navigating without a map. Here's why a strategy is crucial:

Guides Your Decisions: Keeps you aligned with your financial goals.

Prepares You for Volatility: Reduces emotional decision-making during market fluctuations.

Optimizes Your Resources: Ensures your money is working effectively for you.

Key Idea: A good strategy balances risk and reward while adapting to your individual circumstances.

5.2 Setting Your Investment Objectives

Your strategy begins with defining your goals.

Short-Term Objectives: Goals within 1-3 years, such as saving for a home down payment.

Example Strategy: Focus on low-risk investments like bonds or money market funds.

Long-Term Objectives: Goals 10+ years away, such as retirement.

Example Strategy: Emphasize growth investments like stocks and index funds.

Combination Goals: Balancing multiple timelines with diversified portfolios.

Action Step: Write down your objectives and the timeframes for achieving them.

5.3 Determining Your Asset Allocation

Asset allocation is how you distribute your investments among different asset classes, such as stocks, bonds, and cash.

Why It Matters:

Controls the risk-return profile of your portfolio.

Aligns with your financial goals and risk tolerance.

Common Allocation Models:

Aggressive: 80-90% in stocks, 10-20% in bonds/cash.

Moderate: 60-70% in stocks, 30-40% in bonds/cash.

Conservative: 30-50% in stocks, 50-70% in bonds/cash.

Adjusting Over Time:

Shift toward more conservative allocations as you approach retirement.

Example Rule: The "110 Minus Age" Rule – Subtract your age from 110 to determine the percentage of stocks in your portfolio.

Action Step: Choose an asset allocation that reflects your goals and risk tolerance.

5.4 Diversification: Spreading Risk Across Investments

Diversification protects your portfolio by reducing dependence on any single investment.

What to Diversify:

Across Asset Classes: Stocks, bonds, ETFs, real estate, etc.

Within Asset Classes: Invest in different sectors, industries, and geographies.

Why It Works:

A poor-performing investment is offset by better-performing ones.

Example: Tech stocks may fall, but healthcare stocks may rise during a recession.

Action Step: Build a portfolio with a mix of assets and sectors to reduce overall risk.

5.5 Choosing Between Active and Passive Strategies

Active Investing:

Involves frequent buying and selling of stocks to outperform the market.

Requires significant research, time, and expertise.

Example: Stock-picking or investing in actively managed funds.

Passive Investing:

Focuses on matching market performance rather than beating it.

Example: Investing in index funds or ETFs.

Which is Right for You?

Beginners often benefit from passive strategies for simplicity and lower costs.

Action Step: Decide if you prefer hands-on (active) or hands-off (passive) investing.

5.6 Dollar-Cost Averaging: A Beginner-Friendly Approach

What It Is: Investing a fixed amount regularly, regardless of market conditions.

How It Works:

Buys more shares when prices are low and fewer when prices are high.

Reduces the impact of market volatility.

Example: Investing $200 every month in an ETF.

Why It's Effective:

Simplifies investing and removes the temptation to time the market.

Action Step: Set up automatic contributions to implement dollar-cost averaging.

5.7 Rebalancing Your Portfolio

What It Is: Adjusting your portfolio periodically to maintain your desired asset allocation.

Why It's Important:

Prevents overexposure to any one asset class.

Locks in gains and ensures alignment with your risk tolerance.

Example: If stocks grow from 60% to 75% of your portfolio, sell some stocks or add bonds to rebalance.

How Often to Rebalance:

Annually or when allocations deviate significantly from your target.

Action Step: Schedule an annual review to rebalance your portfolio.

5.8 Managing Emotional Traps

Avoid Common Mistakes:

Fear of Missing Out (FOMO): Buying into hype-driven stocks.

Panic Selling: Reacting emotionally to market downturns.

Overconfidence: Taking excessive risks after a few wins.

Strategies to Stay Disciplined:

Focus on long-term goals.

Ignore daily market noise and media sensationalism.

Stick to your plan, even during volatility.

Action Step: Create a checklist to remind yourself of your long-term strategy during market turbulence.

5.9 Case Studies: Real-World Applications

Case Study 1: A Beginner's Growth Portfolio

Investor: 30-year-old saving for retirement.

Strategy: 80% in index funds, 10% in sector ETFs, 10% in bonds.

Outcome: Steady growth over 10 years through dollar-cost averaging.

Case Study 2: A Conservative Approach for a Near-Retiree

Investor: 60-year-old preparing for retirement.

Strategy: 40% in dividend-paying stocks, 40% in bonds, 20% in REITs.

Outcome: Consistent income with minimal risk.

Conclusion:

A well-crafted investment strategy is your blueprint for achieving financial success. By setting clear goals, diversifying your portfolio, and managing emotions, you can navigate the stock market with confidence. In the next chapter, we'll dive into analyzing stocks and reading financial reports to make informed investment decisions.

Chapter 6: Analyzing Stocks – How to Make Informed Investment Decisions

6.1 The Importance of Stock Analysis

Investing in stocks isn't a gamble when you approach it with the right information. Analyzing stocks helps you:

Understand Company Health: Evaluate financial strength and stability.

Assess Growth Potential: Identify opportunities for capital appreciation.

Manage Risk: Avoid overvalued or poorly performing companies.

Key Idea: A good investor is also a good researcher.

6.2 Fundamental Analysis: Digging into the Basics

Fundamental analysis evaluates a company's intrinsic value by examining its financial and business performance.

6.2.1 Understanding Financial Statements

Income Statement (Profit & Loss Statement):

Tracks revenue, expenses, and net income.

Key Metrics: Revenue Growth, Net Profit Margin.

Example: A company with growing revenue and stable margins shows profitability.

Balance Sheet:

Lists a company's assets, liabilities, and shareholder equity.

Key Metrics: Debt-to-Equity Ratio, Current Ratio.

Example: A company with high debt compared to equity may be financially unstable.

Cash Flow Statement:

Shows how cash is generated and used.

Key Metrics: Free Cash Flow, Operating Cash Flow.

Example: Positive cash flow indicates the company can sustain operations and growth.

6.2.2 Key Financial Ratios

Price-to-Earnings (P/E) Ratio:

Measures stock price relative to earnings per share (EPS).

A high P/E may indicate overvaluation; a low P/E could signal a bargain.

Debt-to-Equity (D/E) Ratio:

Compares total debt to shareholder equity.

Lower ratios often suggest financial stability.

Return on Equity (ROE):

Shows how effectively management uses equity to generate profits.

Higher ROE indicates better efficiency.

Action Step: Use free resources like Yahoo Finance or Morningstar to access financial statements and ratios.

6.3 Technical Analysis: Understanding Market Trends

Technical analysis focuses on stock price movements and trading volume to identify patterns.

6.3.1 Common Charts and Patterns

Line Charts: Tracks stock price over time; great for beginners.

Candlestick Charts: Provides detailed information on price movements within a specific period.

Key Patterns:

Head and Shoulders: Indicates potential trend reversal.

Double Bottom: Suggests a bullish (upward) reversal.

6.3.2 Popular Technical Indicators

Moving Averages:

Simple Moving Average (SMA) smooths out price data for a clearer trend view.

Example: The 50-day SMA crossing above the 200-day SMA is often a bullish signal.

Relative Strength Index (RSI):

Measures overbought or oversold conditions (scale of 0-100).

RSI above 70: Stock may be overbought. RSI below 30: Stock may be oversold.

Volume Analysis:

Rising volume confirms the strength of a price trend.

Action Step: Use platforms like TradingView to practice reading charts and applying technical indicators.

6.4 Qualitative Analysis: Beyond the Numbers

Look at factors that affect a company's long-term success but aren't always reflected in financial data.

6.4.1 Management and Leadership

Assess the experience, reputation, and track record of company executives.

Example: A CEO with a history of successful turnarounds can indicate strong leadership.

6.4.2 Competitive Advantage (Moat)

Companies with unique products, brand loyalty, or cost advantages often outperform competitors.

Example: Coca-Cola's global brand recognition is a significant competitive advantage.

6.4.3 Industry Trends

Identify growing industries and companies well-positioned to benefit.
Example: Renewable energy is expected to grow significantly in the next decade.

Action Step: Read annual reports and industry news to understand qualitative factors.

6.5 Evaluating Stock Valuation

Determining whether a stock is overvalued, undervalued, or fairly valued helps guide buying decisions.

6.5.1 Intrinsic Value Approach

Calculate the present value of a company's future cash flows.

Tools: Discounted Cash Flow (DCF) analysis.

6.5.2 Relative Valuation Approach

Compare a stock's metrics (e.g., P/E ratio) to peers or industry averages.

Example: If Company A's P/E is 15 and the industry average is 20, it may be undervalued.

6.5.3 Market Sentiment Approach

Consider broader market conditions influencing stock prices.

Example: Stocks often become undervalued during recessions due to fear-based selling.

Action Step: Use online calculators and analyst reports to estimate valuations.

6.6 Tools for Stock Analysis

Leverage technology and resources to simplify stock analysis.

Free Tools:

Yahoo Finance: Financial statements and market data.

Google Finance: Simplified performance tracking.

Premium Tools:

Morningstar: In-depth research reports and ratings.

Bloomberg Terminal: Advanced analytics (best for professionals).

Educational Resources:

Books: The Intelligent Investor by Benjamin Graham.

Online Courses: Platforms like Udemy or Coursera offer beginner-friendly courses.

Action Step: Choose one or two tools to start practicing stock analysis.

6.7 Case Study: Analyzing a Real Stock

Stock: Apple Inc. (AAPL).

Step 1: Review Financial Statements:

Revenue Growth: Consistent growth over the past 5 years.

Net Profit Margin: Strong at 25%, reflecting efficiency.

Step 2: Apply Ratios:

P/E Ratio: 28 (higher than the industry average, suggesting premium valuation).

ROE: 30% (indicates efficient use of equity).

Step 3: Assess Qualitative Factors:

Strong brand loyalty and a diversified product portfolio.

Leadership under Tim Cook has maintained innovation.

Conclusion: While Apple is a strong performer, its valuation suggests limited upside unless future growth accelerates.

Conclusion

Analyzing stocks involves a blend of quantitative and qualitative evaluation. By mastering these techniques, you can make well-informed investment decisions and build a portfolio tailored to your goals. In the next chapter, we'll explore risk management strategies to safeguard your investments.

Chapter 7: Managing Risk and Diversifying Your Portfolio

7.1 Understanding Investment Risk

Risk is an inherent part of investing, but understanding it empowers you to manage it effectively.

7.1.1 Types of Risk

Market Risk: The risk of losses due to overall market movements (e.g., stock market downturns).

Credit Risk: The risk of a bond issuer defaulting on payments.

Liquidity Risk: Difficulty in selling an investment without impacting its price significantly.

Inflation Risk: The risk of inflation eroding your investment's purchasing power.

Interest Rate Risk: The impact of changing interest rates, especially on bonds.

7.1.2 Risk Tolerance

Your risk tolerance determines how much fluctuation in value you can handle.

Low Risk Tolerance: Focus on bonds and stable assets.

High Risk Tolerance: More comfortable with stocks and volatile markets.

Action Step: Take an online risk tolerance questionnaire to better understand your comfort level with risk.

7.2 The Role of Diversification in Reducing Risk

Diversification spreads your investments across different asset classes, sectors, and geographies to reduce risk.

7.2.1 Diversifying Across Asset Classes

Stocks: Provide growth but are more volatile.

Bonds: Offer stability and income, counterbalancing stock volatility.

Real Estate (REITs): Adds another layer of diversification with potential for steady returns.

Cash Equivalents: Low-risk assets like money market funds for liquidity.

7.2.2 Diversifying Within Asset Classes

Stocks: Invest in different sectors (technology, healthcare, energy, etc.) and geographies (domestic vs. international).

Bonds: Include a mix of government, municipal, and corporate bonds.

Example: A portfolio might allocate 60% to stocks (split across tech, healthcare, and energy), 30% to bonds (split between corporate and government), and 10% to REITs.

Action Step: Review your portfolio to ensure it is diversified across sectors and regions.

7.3 Managing Volatility

Volatility refers to the degree of variation in an asset's price over time.

7.3.1 Strategies to Manage Volatility

Invest Regularly: Use dollar-cost averaging to mitigate the impact of price swings.

Focus on Long-Term Goals: Short-term fluctuations are less significant over longer periods.

Avoid Overconcentration: Ensure no single stock or sector dominates your portfolio.

7.3.2 Handling Market Corrections

What is a Correction? A decline of 10% or more in a stock or market index.

How to Respond:

Revisit your long-term strategy rather than panic selling.

Consider buying undervalued stocks during corrections.

Action Step: Create a checklist for handling volatility, such as reviewing long-term goals before making decisions.

7.4 Hedging Strategies

Hedging involves using investments to offset potential losses in your portfolio.

7.4.1 Common Hedging Tools

Options: Use puts and calls to protect against price drops or lock in prices.

Inverse ETFs: Gain when the market declines.

Commodities: Gold and other commodities often act as a hedge against inflation and market instability.

Example: Buying a put option for a stock in your portfolio can limit losses if the stock price falls.

Action Step: Research basic options strategies or consult with a financial advisor before implementing hedging tools.

7.5 The Role of Asset Allocation

Asset allocation balances risk and reward by dividing your portfolio among different asset classes.

7.5.1 Allocation Models

Aggressive: High exposure to stocks (e.g., 80% stocks, 20% bonds) for long-term growth.

Moderate: Balanced mix of stocks and bonds (e.g., 60% stocks, 40% bonds).

Conservative: Focused on preserving capital (e.g., 40% stocks, 60% bonds).

7.5.2 Adjusting Your Allocation Over Time

Reduce stock exposure and increase bonds as you near retirement.

Example: Shift from 80% stocks and 20% bonds at age 30 to 40% stocks and 60% bonds at age 60.

Action Step: Choose an allocation model based on your goals, risk tolerance, and time horizon.

7.6 Creating an Emergency Fund

An emergency fund provides a financial safety net and prevents you from dipping into investments.

7.6.1 How Much to Save

3-6 months of living expenses.

For higher-risk professions or volatile incomes, aim for 6-12 months.

7.6.2 Where to Keep It

High-yield savings accounts or money market funds.

Ensure the fund is easily accessible and low-risk.

Action Step: Calculate your monthly expenses and set up automatic transfers to build your emergency fund.

7.7 Monitoring and Rebalancing Your Portfolio

Rebalancing ensures your portfolio remains aligned with your target asset allocation.

7.7.1 When to Rebalance

Scheduled Rebalancing: Annually or semi-annually.

Threshold Rebalancing: When an asset class exceeds a set deviation (e.g., 5-10% off target).

7.7.2 How to Rebalance

Sell overperforming assets or add funds to underperforming ones.

Example: If stocks grow from 60% to 70% of your portfolio, sell some stocks and buy bonds to restore balance.

Action Step: Set a calendar reminder to review your portfolio regularly.

7.8 Case Study: Managing Risk in a Real Portfolio

Investor: 40-year-old saving for retirement with moderate risk tolerance.

Portfolio Before Diversification:

80% in tech stocks, 20% in bonds.

Diversified Portfolio:

60% stocks (tech, healthcare, consumer goods), 30% bonds (corporate and government), 10% REITs.

Rebalancing Example:

After 1 year, stocks grow to 70%. Rebalancing restores the allocation to 60% stocks and 30% bonds.

Outcome: Reduced risk and improved stability without sacrificing growth potential.

Conclusion

Risk management and diversification are cornerstones of successful investing. By spreading investments across asset classes and regularly monitoring your portfolio, you can protect yourself from excessive losses while staying on track toward your financial goals. In the next chapter, we'll explore the power of staying disciplined and investing consistently to build long-term wealth.

Chapter 8:
The Power of
Consistency –
Building Long-Term
Wealth

8.1 The Importance of Consistency in Investing

Building wealth is not about timing the market; it's about staying disciplined and investing consistently.

Key Idea: Small, regular investments can grow significantly over time due to the power of compounding.

Example: Investing $200 per month for 30 years at an 8% annual return yields approximately $300,000, even though you only contributed $72,000.

8.2 The Role of Dollar-Cost Averaging (DCA)

Dollar-cost averaging involves investing a fixed amount regularly, regardless of market conditions.

8.2.1 Benefits of DCA

Reduces Emotional Decision-Making: Avoids the urge to time the market.

Buys More Shares When Prices Are Low: This averages out the cost of shares over time.

Encourages Discipline: Builds a habit of consistent investing.

Example:

Investor A contributes $500 monthly to an index fund. When prices are low, they buy more shares; when prices are high, they buy fewer. Over time, their average cost per share remains steady and lower than irregular lump-sum investments.

Action Step: Set up automatic contributions to your investment account.

8.3 Leveraging Compounding to Maximize Returns

Compounding occurs when your investments generate earnings, and those earnings are reinvested to generate even more.

8.3.1 Factors Influencing Compounding

Time: The longer your money stays invested, the greater the compounding effect.

Rate of Return: Higher returns accelerate growth.

Consistency: Regular contributions amplify compounding.

Example of Compounding Growth:

Invest $10,000 at an 8% annual return. After:
10 years: $21,589.
20 years: $46,610.
30 years: $100,627.

Action Step: Use a compounding calculator to see how your investments can grow over time.

8.4 Staying the Course During Market Fluctuations

Markets are unpredictable, but maintaining consistency during downturns is key to long-term success.

8.4.1 Historical Context

Example: During the 2008 financial crisis, the S&P 500 dropped 37%, but investors who stayed invested saw significant recovery in the following years.

Lesson: Market dips are opportunities for disciplined investors to buy at lower prices.

8.4.2 Avoiding Panic Selling

Selling during downturns locks in losses and prevents you from benefiting from the recovery. Instead, focus on your long-term plan and ignore short-term noise.

Action Step: Create a "stay-the-course" checklist to review during market volatility.

8.5 Automating Your Investments

Automation simplifies the investing process and ensures consistency.

8.5.1 Benefits of Automation

Eliminates Forgetfulness: Regular contributions happen without manual effort.

Reduces Emotional Influence: Automation helps you stick to your plan during market highs and lows.

8.5.2 How to Automate Investments

Set up direct transfers from your paycheck or bank account to your investment account.

Use robo-advisors or investment apps to automatically allocate funds according to your strategy.

Action Step: Research platforms like Vanguard, Fidelity, or Betterment to automate your investments.

8.6 Setting and Adjusting Goals Over Time

Consistency doesn't mean rigidity; your investment plan should adapt as your goals and circumstances change.

8.6.1 Life Events That May Impact Goals

Marriage or Divorce: Changes in household income or financial priorities.

Career Changes: Fluctuations in salary may require adjusting contributions.

Retirement Planning: Shift focus from growth to income generation as retirement nears.

8.6.2 Reviewing Your Progress

Assess your portfolio's performance annually.

Check if your investments align with your current risk tolerance and financial goals.

Action Step: Schedule an annual review of your portfolio and financial goals.

8.7 The Long-Term Mindset

Wealth-building takes time, patience, and a focus on the big picture.

8.7.1 Avoiding Get-Rich-Quick Schemes

Investments promising unusually high returns are often risky or fraudulent.
Stick with proven, steady growth strategies like index funds or ETFs.

8.7.2 The Power of Patience

Example: Warren Buffett made most of his wealth after age 50 due to the compounding effect.

Lesson: The earlier you start and the longer you stay invested, the greater your returns.

8.7.3 Focus on Progress, Not Perfection

Consistency doesn't mean never making mistakes—it means learning and improving over time.

8.8 Case Study: Consistent Investing Over 20 Years

Investor: 25-year-old starts investing $400 per month in an S&P 500 index fund.

Outcome:

By age 45, with an 8% average annual return, their portfolio grows to over $240,000.

If they stop contributing and let it grow until age 65, it becomes over $1,100,000.

Conclusion

Consistency is the foundation of successful investing. By automating contributions, staying disciplined during market volatility, and focusing on long-term goals, you can harness the power of compounding to build lasting wealth. In the next chapter, we'll explore tax strategies and other ways to maximize your investment returns.

Chapter 9:
Tax Strategies and Maximizing Investment Returns

9.1 Understanding the Tax Implications of Investing

Taxes can significantly impact your investment returns. Knowing how to navigate the tax landscape is key to maximizing profits.

9.1.1 Types of Investment Income

Dividends: Payments from stocks or mutual funds, taxed as ordinary income or at a lower rate if qualified.

Capital Gains: Profits from selling an asset for more than its purchase price.

Short-Term Capital Gains: Assets held for less than one year, taxed at your ordinary income tax rate.

Long-Term Capital Gains: Assets held for more than one year, taxed at lower rates (0%, 15%, or 20%, depending on income).

Interest Income: Income from bonds or savings accounts, usually taxed as ordinary income.

Action Step: Review your investment income sources and classify them by tax treatment.

9.2 Tax-Advantaged Accounts

Certain accounts help reduce or defer taxes, allowing your investments to grow more efficiently.

9.2.1 Retirement Accounts

Traditional IRA/401(k): Contributions are tax-deductible, but withdrawals are taxed in retirement.

Roth IRA/401(k): Contributions are made with after-tax dollars, but withdrawals in retirement are tax-free.

Example: A $6,500 annual Roth IRA contribution invested at an 8% return over 30 years grows to over $780,000—withdrawn tax-free.

9.2.2 Health Savings Account (HSA)

Contributions are tax-deductible, growth is tax-free, and withdrawals for qualified medical expenses are also tax-free.
Can act as a supplemental retirement account if used strategically.

9.2.3 529 Plans

Tax-advantaged accounts for education savings.
Earnings grow tax-free, and withdrawals are tax-free for qualified educational expenses.

Action Step: Open or contribute to a tax-advantaged account aligned with your goals.

9.3 Strategies to Reduce Taxable Income

Reducing taxable income can lower your tax bracket and increase after-tax returns.

9.3.1 Tax-Loss Harvesting

What It Is: Selling investments at a loss to offset taxable gains.

How It Works:

Example: You sell Stock A at a $2,000 loss and Stock B at a $2,000 gain. The loss offsets the gain, so you owe no capital gains tax.
Up to $3,000 in net losses can offset ordinary income annually.

9.3.2 Contribute to Tax-Deferred Accounts

Contributions to 401(k)s, Traditional IRAs, and HSAs reduce your taxable income for the year.

Action Step: Consider reallocating funds in taxable accounts to maximize tax-loss harvesting opportunities.

9.4 Tax-Efficient Investment Strategies

Where you hold certain investments impacts their tax efficiency.

9.4.1 Asset Location

Taxable Accounts: Hold tax-efficient investments like municipal bonds and ETFs.

Tax-Advantaged Accounts: Hold tax-inefficient investments like REITs, high-dividend stocks, and bonds.

9.4.2 Choose Tax-Efficient Investments

Index Funds and ETFs: These have low turnover, minimizing capital gains distributions.

Municipal Bonds: Interest is often tax-free at the federal level and potentially at the state level.

Example: Holding a high-turnover mutual fund in a taxable account might generate unnecessary tax liabilities, while the same fund in an IRA or 401(k) avoids annual taxes.

Action Step: Review your portfolio to ensure investments are in the most tax-advantaged accounts.

9.5 Understanding Required Minimum Distributions (RMDs)

RMDs apply to tax-deferred accounts (like Traditional IRAs) starting at age 73.
Failing to withdraw the required amount results in a 50% tax penalty on the shortfall.

Strategies to Manage RMDs:

Start making withdrawals before RMD age to spread out the tax burden.
Convert Traditional IRAs to Roth IRAs during lower-income years to reduce future RMDs.

Action Step: Use an RMD calculator to estimate your future withdrawal requirements.

9.6 Avoiding Common Tax Mistakes

Being proactive can help avoid costly errors.

9.6.1 Frequent Mistakes

Overlooking Tax-Advantaged Accounts: Not maximizing contributions to 401(k)s or IRAs.

Triggering Wash Sales: Rebuying the same or substantially similar investment within 30 days of a tax-loss sale.

Ignoring State Taxes: Some states have unique rules for capital gains and dividends.

Action Step: Consult a tax professional annually to ensure compliance and optimize your tax strategy.

9.7 Working With a Tax Professional

A professional can help maximize deductions and ensure compliance with changing tax laws.

9.7.1 When to Consult a Professional

If you have significant investment income or complex holdings.
When you're nearing retirement and need RMD planning.

9.7.2 Questions to Ask Your Advisor

How can I reduce my tax liability?

Which accounts should I prioritize for contributions or withdrawals?

Are there any new tax laws that could affect my portfolio?

Action Step: Schedule an annual meeting with a CPA or financial advisor specializing in tax-efficient investing.

9.8 Case Study: Tax Strategies in Action

Investor: A 45-year-old with $500,000 split between a 401(k), a Roth IRA, and a taxable brokerage account.

Problem: High tax bill due to dividends and capital gains distributions from taxable investments.

Solution:

Shift high-dividend and bond investments to the 401(k).

Use index funds and ETFs in the taxable account.

Increase Roth IRA contributions for tax-free withdrawals in retirement.

Outcome: Reduced annual tax liability by $5,000 and maximized long-term growth.

Conclusion

Taxes can erode investment returns, but with the right strategies, you can minimize their impact and keep more of your earnings. In the final chapter, we'll bring it all together with actionable tips for maintaining discipline, avoiding pitfalls, and achieving your financial goals.

Chapter 10: Bringing It All Together – Your Roadmap to Investment Success

10.1 Reviewing the Investment Journey

Let's revisit the major concepts covered in this book and understand how they interconnect.

10.1.1 The Foundation

The stock market provides a platform for wealth building by investing in businesses.

Developing a strong financial foundation through budgeting, emergency funds, and eliminating debt is crucial before investing.

10.1.2 The Strategy

Begin with clear, measurable goals.
Diversify your portfolio to manage risk and use asset allocation tailored to your age, income, and risk tolerance.

10.1.3 The Process

Regularly contribute to your investment accounts, leveraging automation.

Reassess your investments periodically but avoid overreacting to short-term market movements.

Action Step: Write down your personal investment strategy based on the principles from earlier chapters.

10.2 Crafting Your Personalized Investment Plan

A well-thought-out plan is the roadmap to achieving your financial goals.

10.2.1 Define Your Goals

Short-Term Goals: E.g., saving for a house down payment.

Long-Term Goals: E.g., building a retirement fund or funding education for children.

10.2.2 Identify Your Time Horizon

Short-term goals might require conservative investments.

Long-term goals benefit from growth-focused strategies like equity investments.

10.2.3 Choose Your Investment Mix

Combine stocks, bonds, ETFs, and other assets in proportions that align with your goals and risk tolerance.

Use target-date funds if you want a hands-off approach.

10.2.4 Automate Contributions

Set up recurring transfers to investment accounts to ensure consistency.

Action Step: Create a one-page summary of your personalized investment plan and keep it as a reference.

10.3 Avoiding Common Pitfalls

Learning from the mistakes of others can save you time, money, and stress.

10.3.1 Emotional Decision-Making

Avoid buying when the market is at its peak or selling during downturns.
Stick to your strategy and focus on long-term goals.

10.3.2 Neglecting to Rebalance

Periodically adjust your portfolio to maintain your desired asset allocation.

Example: If stocks outperform and grow to 70% of your portfolio when your target is 60%, sell some stocks and buy bonds to rebalance.

10.3.3 Overlooking Fees and Expenses

High fees can erode returns over time.

Opt for low-cost funds like ETFs and index funds.

Action Step: Create a checklist of potential pitfalls to review annually and ensure you're staying on track.

10.4 Embracing a Long-Term Perspective

Wealth-building is a marathon, not a sprint.

10.4.1 The Role of Patience

Short-term volatility is a natural part of investing.

Markets have historically trended upward over the long term despite occasional downturns.

10.4.2 Trust the Power of Compounding

Regular investments over time, coupled with reinvesting returns, create exponential growth.

Example: A $10,000 investment earning 8% annually doubles roughly every 9 years. Over 36 years, it grows to $160,000.

10.5 Staying Educated and Informed

The investment world evolves, and staying informed is essential.

10.5.1 Resources to Keep Learning

Books: Read classics like The Intelligent Investor by Benjamin Graham.

Websites and Blogs: Follow trusted financial platforms for updates and tips.

Courses: Take online courses to deepen your understanding of investing.

10.5.2 Seek Professional Guidance When Needed

Work with a certified financial planner or investment advisor to tailor your strategy.

Action Step: Commit to reading at least one investment-related book or taking one course each year.

10.6 Taking Action: Your First 90 Days

Start strong with an actionable plan for the first three months of your investment journey.

10.6.1 Month 1: Build Your Foundation

Set up a budget to free up money for investing.

Open a brokerage account or retirement account.

Define your goals and choose an asset allocation.

10.6.2 Month 2: Begin Investing

Fund your account and make your first investments, focusing on diversified options like index funds or ETFs.

Set up automation for regular contributions.

10.6.3 Month 3: Review and Adjust

Evaluate your portfolio to ensure it aligns with your goals.

Make minor adjustments as needed but avoid overtrading.

Action Step: Use a calendar or task tracker to follow through on your 90-day plan.

10.7 Final Words of Encouragement

Investing is a journey that requires discipline, patience, and a commitment to growth.

10.7.1 Acknowledging Progress

Celebrate milestones like your first investment, reaching your first $10,000, or achieving a financial goal.

10.7.2 The Reward of Persistence

Building wealth through investing is one of the most empowering things you can do for your future.

10.7.3 Remember Your "Why"

Stay motivated by keeping your goals front and center. Whether it's retiring comfortably, funding a child's education, or achieving financial independence, your "why" will keep you on track.

Conclusion

This book has given you the tools to embark on your investment journey with confidence. By applying what you've learned, staying consistent, and continually growing your knowledge, you can achieve your financial goals and create a secure future.

Conclusion

Congratulations! You've made it to the end of this guide, and in doing so, you've taken a significant step toward achieving financial independence and building long-term wealth. By now, you should have a clear understanding of the fundamentals of stock market investing, including how it works, the types of investments available, and the strategies that can help you make informed decisions.

Remember, investing in the stock market isn't a get-rich-quick scheme—it's about consistent, thoughtful decisions over time. The most successful investors are not those who chase trends or try to time the market, but those who focus on long-term growth, manage risk appropriately, and remain patient in the face of market fluctuations.

As you continue on your investing journey, keep in mind the following key takeaways:

Start Simple: Begin with diversified, low-cost investments like index funds or ETFs. This helps reduce risk while you build your understanding of the market.

Invest for the Long-Term: The stock market rewards patience. Resist the urge to make impulsive decisions based on short-term market movements.

Stay Educated: The world of investing is always evolving. Keep learning, whether through books, articles, courses, or by simply observing the market. The more informed you are, the better decisions you can make.

Develop a Strategy and Stick to It: Having a clear investment plan, based on your goals and risk tolerance, is crucial. Don't let emotions dictate your investment choices.

Consistency is Key: Regular contributions, even small ones, can grow significantly over time thanks to the power of compound interest.

Your journey doesn't end here. In fact, it's just the beginning. As you continue to build your portfolio and grow your understanding of the market, you'll develop your own strategies and refine your approach. The world of investing is open to anyone willing to learn, and you've already taken the most important first step.

Whether you're investing to save for retirement, to achieve financial independence, or to reach specific financial milestones, the key is to stay disciplined, stay informed, and keep moving forward. The stock market will have its ups and downs, but with the right mindset and strategy, you can navigate those fluctuations and work toward achieving your financial goals.

Thank you for joining me on this journey. I wish you success as you embark on your path to becoming a confident, knowledgeable investor. Your financial future is in your hands— now go ahead and take the next step!

Glossary of Stock Market Terms

1. Asset Allocation
The process of dividing your investment portfolio among different asset categories, such as stocks, bonds, and cash, to balance risk and reward based on your goals, time horizon, and risk tolerance.

2. Bear Market
A market condition where prices of securities are falling or are expected to fall, typically by 20% or more from recent highs.

3. Blue-Chip Stocks
Shares of well-established, financially stable, and reputable companies with a history of reliable performance, such as Apple or Coca-Cola.

4. Bond
A fixed-income investment that represents a loan made by an investor to a borrower, typically a corporation or government, with regular interest payments and return of the principal at maturity.

5. Bull Market
A market condition where prices of securities are rising or are expected to rise, often fueled by investor confidence and economic growth.

6. Capital Gains
The profit earned from the sale of an investment when the sale price exceeds the purchase price.

7. Dividend
A portion of a company's earnings distributed to shareholders, typically on a regular basis (e.g., quarterly).

8. Dollar-Cost Averaging (DCA)
An investment strategy where you regularly invest a fixed amount of money in a particular asset, regardless of its price, to reduce the impact of market volatility.

9. Earnings Per Share (EPS)
A company's profit divided by the number of outstanding shares of its stock. A key metric used to evaluate a company's profitability.

10. Exchange-Traded Fund (ETF)
A type of investment fund traded on stock exchanges that holds a basket of assets, such as stocks or bonds, and is designed to track the performance of a specific index.

11. Index Fund
A mutual fund or ETF designed to replicate the performance of a specific market index, such as the S&P 500.

12. Initial Public Offering (IPO)
The first time a company offers its shares to the public, transitioning from private to public ownership.

13. Liquidity
The ease with which an asset can be bought or sold in the market without affecting its price. Stocks and ETFs are highly liquid, whereas real estate is less so.

14. Market Capitalization (Market Cap)
The total value of a company's outstanding shares, calculated by multiplying the current stock price by the total number of shares.

15. Mutual Fund
An investment vehicle that pools money from multiple investors to buy a diversified portfolio of stocks, bonds, or other securities.

16. Portfolio
A collection of investments, such as stocks, bonds, ETFs, and cash, owned by an individual or institution.

17. Price-to-Earnings (P/E) Ratio
A valuation metric calculated by dividing a company's current stock price by its earnings per share. It indicates how much investors are willing to pay for $1 of earnings.

18. Rebalancing
The process of adjusting the weightings of assets in your portfolio to maintain your desired level of asset allocation, typically done periodically.

19. Risk Tolerance
The level of risk an investor is willing to accept when making investment decisions, influenced by factors like financial goals, time horizon, and personal comfort with volatility.

20. Roth IRA
A tax-advantaged retirement account where contributions are made with after-tax dollars, and withdrawals in retirement are tax-free.

21. S&P 500
A stock market index that tracks the performance of 500 of the largest companies in the U.S. by market capitalization.

22. Stock
A type of security that represents ownership in a corporation, entitling the holder to a portion of the company's profits and assets.

23. Target-Date Fund
A mutual fund or ETF that automatically adjusts its asset allocation to become more conservative as a specified target date, such as retirement, approaches.

24. Time Horizon
The length of time an investor expects to hold an investment to achieve a financial goal, ranging from short-term (less than 3 years) to long-term (10 years or more).

25. Volatility
The degree of variation in the price of a security or market over time. High volatility indicates larger price swings, while low volatility signifies stability.

26. Yield
The income return on an investment, expressed as a percentage. For stocks, it's typically the dividend yield; for bonds, it's the interest yield.

Software Equipment & Supplies Needed to Get Started

Here's a list of software, equipment, and supplies to help you get started in stock market investing. These tools and resources will streamline your workflow, ensure you stay organized, and enhance your decision-making.

Software

1. Trading Platforms

Robinhood (Beginner-friendly, commission-free trades).
E*TRADE (Comprehensive tools for both beginners and experienced traders).
Fidelity (Excellent for long-term investors, includes research tools).
TD Ameritrade (Offers advanced features with its thinkorswim platform).
Webull (Commission-free trading with advanced charts).

2. Portfolio Management Tools

Morningstar Portfolio Manager: Track, analyze, and rebalance your portfolio.
Personal Capital: Combines budgeting and portfolio analysis for a holistic financial view.
Yahoo Finance Portfolio: Free and easy-to-use portfolio tracking.

3. Research and Analysis Tools

Stock Rover: Detailed analytics, comparison tools, and portfolio tracking.
Zacks Investment Research: Provides stock analysis and recommendations.
Seeking Alpha: Community-driven research and analysis.

4. Charting and Technical Analysis

TradingView: Advanced charting software with customizable indicators.
MetaStock: Comprehensive technical analysis software for active traders.

5. Tax and Accounting Software

TurboTax Premier: Tailored for investors to track and report gains and losses.
H&R Block Tax Software: Includes tools for stock market investors.

6. Educational Platforms

Coursera: Investment courses from universities like Yale and Wharton.
Udemy: Affordable courses on stock market basics and trading strategies.
Investopedia Academy: Courses specifically for stock market beginners.

Equipment

1. Computer or Laptop

Investing requires a reliable computer for research, trading, and analysis. Consider:

Apple MacBook Pro: Known for reliability and long battery life.
Dell XPS 15: Powerful performance for multitasking.
Lenovo ThinkPad: Great for budget-conscious investors.

2. Smartphone or Tablet

Mobile access is essential for on-the-go trading and portfolio management. Recommended devices:

Apple iPhone or iPad: Compatible with most trading apps.
Samsung Galaxy Series: Android alternative with powerful features.

3. External Monitors

For tracking multiple stocks and charts simultaneously.

   Dell UltraSharp U2723QE: High-resolution display for detailed analysis.
   LG UltraWide Monitor: Great for multitasking with multiple windows.

4. Backup Storage

Keep your investment data safe.

   Seagate External Hard Drive: For backups of financial documents.
   Cloud Storage (Google Drive or Dropbox): Secure online storage for easy access.

5. Internet Connection

A high-speed internet connection is critical for real-time market data.

   Fiber-optic connections: Recommended for fast and stable speeds.

Supplies

1. Notebooks or Journals

Keep track of investment strategies, notes, and lessons learned.

   Rocketbook Smart Notebook: Reusable and integrates with cloud storage.
   Moleskine Journal: A classic choice for handwritten notes.

2. Organizational Supplies

   File Organizer: Store printed statements, contracts, and tax documents.
   Label Maker: Organize physical records for quick access.

3. Backup Power Supplies

Portable Power Bank: For charging devices during power outages.
Uninterruptible Power Supply (UPS): Protects your computer during sudden outages.

4. Desk Setup

Adjustable Standing Desk: For comfort during long trading hours.
Ergonomic Chair: Reduces strain during extended periods of research.

5. Calculator or Financial Tools

HP 12C Financial Calculator: Specifically designed for financial calculations.
Casio fx-991EX: A versatile, budget-friendly option.

Subscriptions and Services

1. News and Data Services

The Wall Street Journal: Business and financial news.
Bloomberg Terminal: High-end service for real-time data (best for advanced investors).
Yahoo Finance Premium: Offers advanced tools and ad-free experience.

2. Market Alerts

Google Alerts: Custom alerts for specific stocks or sectors.

Morningstar Alerts: Notifications on portfolio performance and updates.

3. Financial Advisors

Consider consulting with a Certified Financial Planner (CFP) to create a solid investment strategy.

Miscellaneous

Whiteboard or Bulletin Board: Visualize strategies, goals, or watchlists.

Headphones with Mic: For online courses, webinars, or virtual advisor consultations.

Coffee Maker or Snacks: Stay energized during long trading sessions!

Priority List of Essentials to Begin Investing

Here's a streamlined list of essentials to help you get started efficiently and without unnecessary expenses:

1. Trading and Portfolio Management Software

These tools will enable you to trade, track investments, and manage your portfolio:

Trading Platform: Start with a beginner-friendly, commission-free platform like Robinhood or Fidelity.

Portfolio Tracker: Use Yahoo Finance Portfolio (free) or Personal Capital for portfolio tracking and analysis.

2. Reliable Computer or Laptop

A mid-range laptop is sufficient for most beginners. Consider options like:

Lenovo ThinkPad (budget-friendly and reliable).

Dell XPS 15 (for more power and multitasking).

3. Smartphone or Tablet

For mobile trading and alerts:

Apple iPhone or Samsung Galaxy Series (compatible with most trading apps).

4. Internet Connection

High-speed internet (fiber-optic if possible) to ensure real-time access to market data and trading platforms.

5. Educational Resources

Invest time in learning with these affordable options:

Book: The Little Book of Common Sense Investing by John C. Bogle.

Online Course: Investing for Beginners on Coursera or Udemy.

Website: Regularly visit Investopedia for easy-to-understand definitions and guides.

6. A Journal for Notes

Keep track of your investment strategies, learnings, and decisions:

Rocketbook Smart Notebook (reusable and connects to cloud storage).
Or simply use a standard Moleskine Notebook.

7. File Organizer

To store and manage important documents like trade confirmations, tax forms, and account statements.

Expandable File Organizer (compact and portable).

8. Backup Power and Data Storage

For safety and reliability:

Portable Power Bank: Keeps your smartphone or tablet charged.

Cloud Storage: Free options like Google Drive or Dropbox for backing up important files.

9. Market News Subscription

Stay informed on the latest market trends and updates:

Free Option: Yahoo Finance or Google Alerts.

Paid Option: A subscription to The Wall Street Journal or Morningstar Premium.

10. Beginner-Friendly Calculations Tool

If you want to calculate returns or understand financial metrics:

Use the free Built-In Calculator on your smartphone or a simple Casio Calculator.

11. Comfortable Workspace

For extended periods of research and trading:

Ergonomic Chair: Prioritize comfort.

Desk Space: A simple table or desk will suffice initially.

12. Optional Add-Ons (When Ready)

As you grow, consider these additions:

External Monitor: Makes multitasking easier (e.g., LG UltraWide Monitor).

Advanced Charting Tools: TradingView for technical analysis (free version available).

Tax Software: Use TurboTax Premier during tax season to simplify reporting.

Next Steps

Open a brokerage account (e.g., Robinhood or Fidelity).

Build a watchlist of stocks or ETFs you're interested in.

Allocate a small amount of capital (what you can afford to lose) and start with index funds or ETFs.

Commit to learning daily with educational content.

Resources

Here's a curated list of resources to help you deepen your knowledge and continue growing as an investor:

Books

The Intelligent Investor by Benjamin Graham
A classic guide to value investing and understanding market principles.

A Random Walk Down Wall Street by Burton Malkiel
Covers a wide range of investing topics and advocates for low-cost index funds.

Common Sense on Mutual Funds by John C. Bogle
Written by the founder of Vanguard, this book explains the benefits of index fund investing.

The Little Book of Common Sense Investing by John C. Bogle
A concise and practical introduction to index investing.

One Up on Wall Street by Peter Lynch
Explores how everyday investors can identify opportunities and invest successfully.

The Psychology of Money by Morgan Housel
Focuses on the behavioral aspects of investing and financial decision-making.

Rich Dad Poor Dad by Robert Kiyosaki
Offers a mindset shift toward wealth-building and financial independence.

The Bogleheads' Guide to Investing by Taylor Larimore, Mel Lindauer, and Michael LeBoeuf
A straightforward guide to low-cost, long-term investing.

Websites and Blogs

Investopedia (investopedia.com)
Comprehensive resource for investing terminology, concepts, and tutorials.

Morningstar (morningstar.com)
Provides insights on mutual funds, ETFs, and individual stocks.

The Motley Fool (fool.com)
Investment news, advice, and stock analysis for beginners and experienced investors.

Seeking Alpha (seekingalpha.com)
Articles and opinions from a wide range of investors and analysts.

Bogleheads Forum (bogleheads.org)
A community dedicated to discussing index investing and personal finance.

Yahoo Finance (finance.yahoo.com)
News, stock quotes, and investment tools for staying informed.

CNBC (cnbc.com)
Real-time market updates and financial news.

Podcasts

The Investing for Beginners Podcast
Simplifies complex investing concepts for those just starting out.

We Study Billionaires (The Investor's Podcast Network)
Features lessons from some of the world's greatest investors.

The Motley Fool Money Show
Offers analysis of current market trends and investment strategies.

BiggerPockets Money Podcast
Focuses on personal finance and wealth-building strategies.

Animal Spirits Podcast
Covers market trends, personal finance, and behavioral finance in an approachable way.

Online Courses

Coursera (coursera.org)
"Investing for Beginners: A Comprehensive Guide" (offered by top universities).

Udemy (udemy.com)
"Stock Market Investing for Beginners" – Accessible and affordable for new investors.

Khan Academy (khanacademy.org)
"Personal Finance" – Includes lessons on investing basics.

Morningstar Investing Classroom
Free interactive courses on mutual funds, ETFs, stocks, and portfolio building.

Skillshare (skillshare.com)
Courses on investing basics and financial literacy from experienced instructors.

Apps and Tools

Yahoo Finance App
Track market data, news, and your portfolio performance.

Morningstar Portfolio Manager
Analyze and monitor your investments in real-time.

Personal Capital
Helps with budgeting, investment tracking, and retirement planning.

Robinhood Learn
Offers free educational resources for beginner investors.

Fidelity or Vanguard Platforms
Many brokerage accounts have free tools, calculators, and educational content.

YouTube Channels

Graham Stephan
Personal finance and investing advice for beginners.

Andrei Jikh
Simplifies investing concepts with a focus on long-term strategies.

Joseph Carlson Show
Portfolio reviews and insights on dividend and value investing.

The Plain Bagel
Explains complex financial topics in an easy-to-understand manner.

Financial Education
Tips for navigating the stock market and building wealth.

Next Steps:

Select one or two books and start reading.

Bookmark a few websites for regular updates.

Subscribe to a podcast or YouTube channel that aligns with your learning style.

Consider taking an online course to strengthen your knowledge base.

We want to thank you for the purchase of this book and more importantly, thank you for reading it to the end. We hope your reading experience was pleasurable and that you would inform your family and friends on Facebook, Twitter or other social media.

We would like to continue to provide you with high-quality books, and that end, would you mind leaving us a review on Amazon.com?

Just use the link below, scroll down about 3/4 of the page and you will see images similar to the one below.

We are extremely grateful for your assistance.

Warm Regards,

Brian Mahoney

MahoneyProducts Publishing

You might also enjoy:

How To Get Money for Small Business Start Up: How to Get Massive Money from Crowdfunding, Government Grants and Government Loans

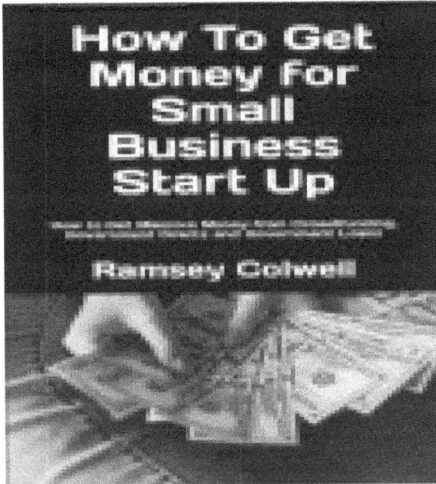

https://rb.gy/9qjcv

or

www.amazon.com/dp/1951929144